OCEAN REFLECTIONS

Meditations to calm your
mind and receive the
wisdom of the ocean

BY
CLAUDIA E. MOORE

CEM Scribe Publishers

Book Cover by CEM Scribe Group LLC

First edition 2025

CONTENTS

INTRODUCTION

There is a rhythm that exists between the ocean and the human soul. Perhaps you have felt it, standing on the shore with your feet sinking into the sand, watching the waves sweep in. In these moments, the ocean speaks to something deep within us, a part of us that longs for peace, calm, and connection. It also offers us profound lessons if we choose to open deeply to it. Those lessons are what inspired me to write this book.

Over the years, I've come to see the ocean not just as a vast body of water, but as a teacher and guide that reflects back to us the truths of life. Whether we are sitting at the water's edge or imagining it from afar, the ocean has the power to calm our minds and open our hearts. Its cycles and mysteries remind us of our own capacity for stillness, presence, and transformation. Through this book, I hope to share the ocean's gifts with you, using meditation as a bridge to deeper awareness.

Ocean Reflections was born from my personal journey of learning to listen to the ocean. I have lived on an ocean's shore for most of my life. While I was living on the Northern California coast, I had the privilege to visit the ocean on a daily basis while I was recovering from a serious illness. The short walk to the beach seemed simple to the external gaze, but no two ocean visits were the same. It was during that time that the content of these meditations came to me, carried on the never-ceasing waves.

This book is meant to be used as a tool for reflection, not just read passively. You may wish to sit by the ocean as you read, allowing the sound of the waves to become a part of your meditation. But if you are far from the sea, do not worry. You can use a recording of the ocean's sounds, watch a video of it, or close your eyes and imagine the waves rolling in. The key is to let the sound and rhythm of water guide you back to a place of calm, where your mind can reflect.

As you read, remember that there is no right or wrong way to engage with these reflections. You may wish to read one meditation a day or spend longer with a particular chapter, letting its ideas wash over you like the tide. The ocean has its own timing, and so does your journey.

We will first contemplate the oceans as a whole, and meditation in general. The specific ocean meditations start in Chapter 3.

CHAPTER ONE

THE OCEANS AS A WHOLE

LET'S CONSIDER THE OCEAN in its full expanse for a moment. The oceans cover over 70% of the Earth's surface. Its vastness is difficult to comprehend. We can imagine the largest land masses we know – perhaps North America, or Australia, or the endless forests of Asia. Those masses are dwarfed by the expanse of the ocean. Despite recent efforts, its depths remain primarily unexplored, and its waves have danced through time long before any of us walked this Earth. It is more than just water; it is a living entity that cradles life itself.

For millennia, the ocean has provided for all of life's needs for thousands of species. From the tiniest plankton to the largest whales, the ocean holds intricate webs of life that exist in perfect balance. Without the ocean, life as we know it would not be possible. It regulates our climate, helps produce the oxygen we breathe, and acts as a massive carbon sink, absorbing harmful emissions that would otherwise overwhelm the atmosphere even more than they already are. Each wave you see, each current that flows, plays a part in maintaining this balance.

Human civilizations have always been drawn to the water. Ancient peoples built their lives around the rhythms of the sea, understanding that its bounty was essential to their survival. They fished its waters, navigated its currents, and used its shores as gateways to exploration and trade. The ocean, with its ceaseless movement and mystery, has profoundly shaped human history.

The oceans also speak to our deepest instincts. Even when we are far from the shore, we feel a pull toward the sea. Perhaps it's the sound of the waves, rhythmic and calming, that calls us back. Or perhaps it's something deeper, the knowledge that the ocean is where life began. We are, in many ways, still connected to the sea. The salt in our bodies mirrors the salt in the ocean's water, a reminder that we carry the ocean within us.

The enormity of the ocean can be both humbling and comforting. In its vastness, we see that we are just a small part of a much bigger picture. The ocean has existed long before us, and it will continue long after we are gone. But in the midst of its timelessness, it invites us to slow down, to breathe, and to remember that we are part of something much greater than ourselves.

As you move through this book, I encourage you to keep the ocean in your awareness, whether you are physically near it or not. Even if you cannot see the ocean from where you are right now, it is always there, influencing the air, the weather, and the life around you. Its presence is constant, like the beating of your heart. And just as the ocean sustains the Earth, it can sustain your spirit. In its endless flow, the ocean reminds us that we, too, are part of this rhythm: connected, sustained, and always moving forward.

Chapter Two

WHAT IS MEDITATION?

M EDITATION, AT ITS ESSENCE, is an act of letting go. It is not about controlling the mind or forcing it into stillness, but rather allowing the mind to soften, like a wave settling gently upon the shore. Meditation is not a rigid discipline requiring intense focus and effort. Rather, it can be a simple, natural practice: of softening your awareness, opening yourself to what is present, and observing the flow of your thoughts, just as you might observe the flow of water.

In the same way that the ocean does not resist its own movement, your mind in meditation becomes receptive. It is a space where you can allow your thoughts to rise and fall without judgment or attachment, like waves rolling in and out. Just like the ocean, your mind may be stormy or calm. Start simply by observing. Notice where your mind goes. This is not a practice of striving, but of deep listening. It invites you to tune in to the quieter, subtler currents that move beneath the surface.

Once you have experienced your mind with that kind of curiosity, you can embark on one of the core principles of meditation: the practice of focusing on a single idea or point of contemplation. This can be a concept, a word, an image, or the breath itself. You bring your awareness to this single point, and if your mind wanders, you simply return, again and again, with the same ease that a wave returns to the shore. The point of focus becomes an anchor, a place to return to when the mind begins to drift. Over time, this practice of observation can create a profound sense of peace. It leads to a calmness that comes not from controlling the mind, but from accepting it as it is.

In the chapters that follow, we will explore specific meditations that draw upon the wisdom of the ocean, including its constancy, interconnectedness, and ability to nourish. These meditations will invite you to focus on a single idea and let that guide your awareness. But always remember: meditation is not about achieving a particular state of mind. It is about allowing your mind to be soft, receptive, and open. It is about observing, without effort, where your mind naturally goes, and allowing that gentle flow to bring you into a deeper sense of peace.

Chapter Three

MEDITATION ON CONSTANCY

THERE IS COMFORT IN the ocean's waves. No matter where you stand, no matter what time of day or season it may be, the waves will always arrive. They rise, they fall, they roll toward the shore, and they pull back again, an unbroken rhythm that has continued for as long as the Earth has existed. This is the essence of constancy. The waves are always there, whether we are watching or not, whether we are thinking of them or not. They continue, undisturbed by our lives, unaffected by the turbulence of our thoughts or the weight of our emotions.

In meditation, the constancy of the waves offers us a profound lesson. Life is filled with ups and downs, moments of joy and moments of struggle. Our inner world is often subject to turmoil, much like the storms that sometimes pass over the ocean. Yet beneath the surface, a steady rhythm and an ongoing flow remain unchanged. The waves of the ocean remind us that, no matter what is happening within or around us, there is always a deeper current of peace that we can return to.

Close your eyes for a moment and imagine yourself standing at the edge of the ocean. Listen to the sound of the waves rolling in, one after another, without pause. Feel their steady, predictable rhythm. In this moment, the waves are not concerned with the challenges you face or the anxieties that may be swirling in your mind. They do not stop for your pain or your joy. They simply continue, rising and falling, as they always have.

This is the lesson of constancy: life, like the waves, continues. There is a rhythm to everything, and no matter how chaotic things may seem on the surface, there is always a deeper flow that moves beneath. The waves do not resist this rhythm; they neither rush nor hesitate. The ocean invites us to embrace the constancy of life, to recognize that even amidst change, there is a steady pulse that remains. There is an unstoppable, deeper flow of life that you can trust.

As you meditate on this idea, allow yourself to tune into your own inner rhythm. Begin by focusing on your breath, the most fundamental rhythm of your body. Like the waves, your breath comes and goes without effort, without force. Inhale, and notice the air filling your lungs. Exhale, and let it go. Just as the ocean's waves are constant, your breath is always with you, carrying you through each moment of your life. No matter what happens, your breath remains a steady companion, reminding you that there is a part of you that is always calm, always present.

The ocean does not pause for the struggles of the shore. The waves continue, regardless of the shifting sands, the winds that blow, or the rocks that stand in their path. In the same way, we can remain steady and calm, regardless of what is happening around us. When life feels overwhelming, remember the waves. Return to your breath, to the steady rhythm that is always with you, and know that you, too, embody a life force that is constant.

The waves of the ocean will continue long after we are gone, just as they have continued long before we arrived. They are unaffected by the small disruptions of life. No matter what you face, the waves continue, and so do you. As you finish this meditation, take a moment to feel gratitude for this wisdom that is always available to us, like the ocean's waves, ready to bring us back to a place of peace and stillness.

Chapter Four

Meditation on Being Inter-Connected

T HE OCEAN IS MORE than just a vast body of water. It is a complex, interconnected web of life and natural forces. Beneath its surface, movement is constant. Currents carry nutrients, tides follow the moon, and a delicate balance of ecosystems thrives in harmony. All the parts of the ocean, from its smallest creatures to its largest inhabitants, are connected in a way that sustains the whole. This intricate dance of life reminds us of the deep interconnectedness that exists not only within the ocean but also within ourselves and the world around us.

When you think of the ocean, picture it as more than just water. It is alive with motion and interaction. The currents sweep through its depths, carrying nutrients from one part of the sea to another. Tiny plankton, the foundation of the ocean's food chain, drift with these currents, feeding creatures both large and small. From the smallest single-celled organisms to the largest of creatures, all life in the ocean is connected through this continuous exchange. The food one creature depends on may be carried across vast distances by the invisible forces of the water, making survival possible for life forms that may never meet, but are still deeply linked.

Even the great whales, the largest creatures on Earth, rely on the tiniest plankton for their sustenance. This interdependence is a reminder that in nature, no being exists in isolation. The ocean, with its complex web of life, teaches us that every part of an ecosystem plays a vital role. Just as the ocean relies on this balance, so too do we rely on the natural world, and each other, for our well-being. In meditation, we can reflect on this truth, allowing ourselves to feel a sense of connection to the world around us.

As you meditate on the concept of interconnectedness, start by focusing your awareness on your breath. Notice how your breath flows in and out, effortlessly connecting you to the air around you. You are connected to the world through each breath. The oxygen you take in is produced by plants, from phytoplankton to vast kelp forests. As on land, the plant life in the ocean plays a crucial role in generating the air we breathe. Even in something as simple as breathing, we are linked to the ocean and to all life on Earth.

This is the nature of interconnectedness: nothing exists in isolation. The ocean interacts constantly with the atmosphere, the winds, the tides, and the gravitational pull of the moon. The ebb and flow of the tides is a direct result of this connection, a gentle reminder that the vast ocean and the moon are inextricably linked. The waves you see at the shore are not just shaped by the water itself, but by the moon's pull, by the wind, and by the shifting temperatures of the atmosphere above.

As you sit with this meditation, imagine yourself floating in the ocean, carried by the currents. These currents, though invisible to you, connect you to every part of the ocean. You are not separate from it; you are a part of its movement. The same water that touches your skin is connected to water miles away, nourishing marine life, interacting with the air, and responding to the moon's cycles. You, too, are a part of this web, linked to the rhythm of life that moves throughout the ocean and the planet.

In your meditation, take a moment to reflect on your own connections. Think of the people in your life, the relationships that sustain you, and the communities you are part of. These connections may not always be visible, but they are always present. They shape your life in subtle and profound ways. We are never truly alone; we are always in relationship with others, even if we cannot see or feel those connections.

This interconnectedness transcends what is immediately apparent. The vast unseen networks of life beneath the surface are proof that many of life's connections are invisible, but powerful nonetheless. Similarly, we are connected to people, places, and experiences in ways that we may not fully understand. A small action, like a wave, can ripple out in ways that affect others far beyond what we can see. This is the beauty of interconnectedness. It reminds us that everything we do, everything we are, is part of a larger whole.

As you end this meditation, bring your awareness back to your breath. Feel the rise and fall of your chest, the gentle rhythm that connects you to life itself. Just as the ocean breathes in its own way, so too do you. Each breath is a reminder of your connection to the world around you, to the oceans, the forests, and all the living beings that share this planet with you.

Chapter Five

MEDITATION ON WORKING WITH OBSTACLES

L ET'S THINK ABOUT THE ocean's waves meeting a jagged coast-
line. As the water approaches the rocks, it does not resist or
avoid them. Instead, it moves with grace, flowing around the obstacle,
embracing the contours of the land. The water is never rigid or stuck.
It is flexible, always finding a way forward. Whether it passes over,
under, around, or through, the water cannot be stopped. It moves
continuously, adapting with ease to whatever lies in its path. In fact, it
is these obstacles that shape the water's flow, creating beautiful, unique
patterns as it moves forward.

In meditation, we too can learn from the way water interacts with
obstacles. Obstacles are a natural part of life, whether they are physical

challenges, emotional difficulties, or mental resistance. At times, we are faced with moments where our path seems blocked, where something stands in the way of where we are trying to go. And yet, just as the water teaches us, these obstacles are not barriers to our progress. They are invitations to adapt, to flow in a new direction, and to find a way through without force or frustration.

Begin your meditation by closing your eyes and imagining yourself as a stream of water. Picture yourself moving gently along a path, flowing smoothly. Now, imagine an obstacle in your way: a rock, a log, or perhaps even a steep drop. As water, you do not resist this obstacle. You do not try to break through it or stop at its edge. Instead, you allow yourself to flow around it, finding the path of least resistance. Feel how naturally and effortlessly you move. You are not stopped by the obstacle, but shaped by it. You may flow to one side, cascade over the top, or seep through a crack. But always, you continue forward.

In life, obstacles often feel like barriers that we must overcome with force. We may believe that the only way through is to push harder, exert more effort, or try to control the situation. However, we can learn to approach obstacles with gentleness and flexibility. When we encounter a difficulty, we can pause, observe, and then find the path that allows us to move forward with ease. Instead of being problems, obstacles can become opportunities to discover new ways of being, new routes we hadn't considered before.

This ability to adapt is a perfect metaphor for resilience. It doesn't fight against the things in its path, but neither does it stop or give up. It moves with patience, with persistence, always seeking the way forward. This is how we can approach our own challenges. When we encounter obstacles in meditation, we can choose to meet them with the same fluidity. We can observe the obstacle, accept its presence, and then gently redirect our attention.

Consider how water reshapes itself when it encounters an obstacle. A large rock in a river creates a shift in the water's movement that can be beautiful to witness. The water's flow is altered, creating a new pattern that would not have existed without the rock's presence. Similarly, the obstacles we face in life often shape us in ways we do not anticipate. They challenge us to grow, to think differently, and to adapt in ways that can ultimately lead to something unexpected and beautiful.

As you continue your meditation, think of a challenge you are facing in your life. Visualize it as a rock in your path that seems immovable. Now, instead of trying to push past it or remove it, imagine yourself as water. How can you flow around this challenge? What new path can you take that allows you to move forward with grace? Just as water finds its way, so too can you. The obstacle does not have to stop you; it can guide you to a new direction, or a new way of thinking or being.

Water, despite its softness, is one of the most powerful forces on Earth. It shapes landscapes, carves canyons, and wears down even the hardest of surfaces. But it does so not through force, but through patience and persistence. Similarly, we can approach the obstacles in our lives with patience and a willingness to adapt. We do not need to force solutions or resist the challenges we face; instead, we can work with them. We can learn to flow around them and to allow them to shape us into something stronger and more resilient.

As you finish this meditation, take a moment to reflect on the obstacles you have faced in your life. How have they shaped you? What new paths have they opened up for you? Obstacles do not have to block our progress. They can guide us toward new ways of being and of growing. Like water, we are resilient, flexible, and always capable of finding a way forward.

Chapter Six

MEDITATION ON RESPONSIVENESS

T HE OCEAN IS NEVER still. Its surface may appear calm, but it is
always alive, always in motion, responding to even the smallest
changes. A gentle breeze stirs ripples across its surface, a school of fish
creates barely perceptible waves as they swim, and the largest inhabitants send currents rolling through its depths. The ocean responds
to everything, from the tiniest disturbance to the grandest forces of
nature. Even the shifting temperature of the air or the movement of
the moon causes the ocean to react, to adjust, to move in harmony with
its surroundings. Nothing is ever fixed or permanent. It is a constant
dance of response, adapting to whatever is present in each moment.

As we sit in meditation, we can learn to cultivate this same responsiveness. Life, like the ocean, is constantly in flux. New challenges,
emotions, and experiences arise, and just as the ocean responds to each

stimulus, we too can respond to the ebb and flow of life with grace and adaptability. The key is not to resist or remain fixed, but to remain open and receptive, responding to whatever comes our way.

Visualize yourself sitting by the ocean, watching its gentle waves. As the wind blows across the surface, you notice how the water responds immediately, effortlessly. The ocean does not hold onto a fixed shape; it moves with the breeze, with the currents beneath, with the life that stirs within it. In the same way, you can allow yourself to respond naturally to whatever arises in your meditation. You don't need to control or force anything. Like the ocean, you can remain open, fluid, and receptive.

Turn your attention to your breath. As you inhale, notice how your body expands slightly. As you exhale, notice how it softens and contracts. Your body, too, is in constant motion, always responding to your breath, your surroundings, and even your thoughts. As you breathe, you are not separate from the world around you; you are part of it. Each breath is a small wave, moving through you, shaping your experience.

In life, we often try to fix things in place, to create a sense of permanence or control. But the ocean teaches us that nothing is ever truly fixed. Even the most solid rocks along the shoreline are eventually shaped by the water's touch. The ocean's responsiveness is its strength, not its weakness. It enables it to adapt, thrive, and maintain balance in an ever-changing world. When we resist change, we create tension and suffering. But when we learn to respond with openness, we find that we can move through life's changes with ease and grace.

As you continue this meditation, bring to mind a situation in your life that feels challenging or uncertain. Perhaps it's something that feels out of your control, such as a difficult emotion or an unexpected event. Now, instead of trying to fix or solve it, imagine yourself responding to it like the ocean responds to a breeze. Feel how you can allow yourself to be flexible, to adjust without resistance. You are not passive, but responsive. You are flowing with the situation rather than fighting against it.

One of the ocean's most profound lessons in responsiveness comes from its relationship with the tides. The moon's gravitational pull creates the rise and fall of the tides, a gentle yet powerful force that the ocean responds to without hesitation. The ocean does not resist the pull of the moon; it flows with it, moving with the rhythms of the universe. In our own lives, we are constantly influenced by circumstances beyond our control, whether physical, emotional, or mental. Instead of resisting these forces, we can learn to move with them, responding to the rhythm of life as it unfolds.

As you conclude this meditation, take a moment to appreciate the wisdom of the ocean's responsiveness. It shows us that nothing is permanent and that change is not something to be feared, but rather something to be embraced. Its ability to respond to even the smallest stimuli is a reminder that we, too, can meet life's challenges with fluidity and openness. In the face of uncertainty or difficulty, we can remember the ocean's lesson: to respond, not with resistance, but with a gentle, flexible spirit that moves with the flow of life.

CHAPTER SEVEN

MEDITATION ON NOURISHMENT

T HE OCEAN IS A giver of life, not only for the creatures within its depths but for the entire planet. Every wave that rolls onto shore carries with it the energy of life and the nutrients that sustain ecosystems. The ocean feeds birds, fish, and countless forms of marine life, which in turn provide sustenance for humans and animals on land. This vast body of water, which covers most of our planet, is not just a passive presence. It actively nurtures, supports, and sustains all living things.

As you begin this meditation, imagine yourself once again standing by the water's edge. The waves come in, one after another, steady and rhythmic. Each wave that crashes onto the shore brings more than just water; it brings life. Feel the subtle but powerful energy of the waves. As they move toward you, they carry with them a gift: ions from the ocean air that refresh and rejuvenate your lungs with every breath. The ocean nourishes not only the physical world but your very being. Breathe in this energy, this nourishment, and allow yourself to be fed by this vast web of life that the ocean supports.

The ocean is the great provider. It feeds life in ways both visible and invisible. Beneath the surface, sunlight filters through the water, reaching forests of seaweed and other marine vegetation. These underwater forests, swaying gently with the currents, form the foundation of the ocean's food chain. They absorb sunlight, converting it into energy, just as plants on land do. This vegetation supports a diverse array of creatures, from the tiny to the large, and in turn, these creatures provide nourishment for other animals, including humans. The ocean is a living, breathing ecosystem where every element plays a part in the cycle of nourishment.

As you meditate, take a moment to reflect on the role the ocean plays in sustaining not just sea life, but all life. The fish that swim in its waters are caught and consumed by humans, providing food for humans around the world. The seaweed that grows in its depths is harvested and used in countless ways, from food to medicine. Even the salt that flavors our meals is a reminder of the ocean's presence in our daily lives. The ocean's nourishment is constant, abundant, and generous, and it reaches far beyond the shoreline.

With each breath, feel the ocean's life-giving energy enter your body. Imagine the charged particles carried by the waves entering your lungs, refreshing and restoring you. The air that flows in from the ocean is rich with energy, purified by its long journey over the open water. Each breath is a gift from the ocean, nourishing your body and mind, connecting you to the natural world in the simplest, most profound way.

The ocean teaches us about abundance. It teaches us that there is always enough; life is constantly being fed and supported. Just as the ocean's currents bring nutrients to life on a vast scale, there is a current of nourishment in your own life, always available to you. You are part of this cycle, a recipient of the ocean's generosity.

As you conclude this meditation, let the image of the ocean's waves remain with you. Allow yourself to feel gratitude for its gifts. It reminds us that we are always being nourished, both physically and spiritually. Embrace this gift, and carry it with you, knowing that the ocean's nourishment is always present, always flowing, always supporting your life and the life of the planet.

Chapter Eight

Meditation on Limitlessness and Abundance

T HE OCEAN STRETCHES ENDLESSLY before you, its horizon merging with the sky, creating the illusion of infinity. No matter how far you look, the water seems to go on forever. This is the nature of the ocean: vast, limitless, and abundant. We name its parts - Pacific, Atlantic, Indian, Arctic - but in truth, all these names are merely boundaries created by the human mind. Beneath the surface, the oceans form a single, continuous body of water, flowing together and inseparable. This is the essence of abundance: there are no real divisions, only the endless, interconnected whole.

In meditation, we are invited to connect with this sense of limit-lessness and to feel the abundance that flows into our lives. The ocean reminds us that there is always more - more water, more life, more energy - circulating through the planet, sustaining all that exists. The ocean's abundance is not something to be measured or contained. It is a cycle that flows endlessly, giving and receiving, always renewing itself.

Begin by imagining yourself standing on the shore, looking out at the ocean. The waves come in, one after another. Yet no matter how many times they crash upon the beach, the ocean remains full, its depths untapped. It offers its water freely, without hesitation or limit. No matter how much is taken from it, the ocean is never diminished. This is the nature of abundance. It is not something that can be exhausted or depleted. It is ever-present, always available, a source that flows endlessly.

As you breathe in, you are inhaling this vastness. With each inhale, you are connected to this infinite abundance. With each exhale, you release any sense of lack, any fear that there is not enough. The ocean reminds you that there is always enough, that life itself is abundant, circling upon itself endlessly.

Just as the different oceans of the world are connected beneath the surface, so too are the many parts of your life linked together. There is no real separation between the different aspects of your being, i.e., your mind, your body, and your spirit. They are all part of the same whole, just as the ocean's currents are all part of the same great body of water. When you meditate on this truth, you begin to see that abundance is not something outside of you, but something that flows through you, just as the ocean flows through the planet.

In life, it is easy to fall into the mindset of scarcity and believe that there is not enough, whether of time, resources, or even love. But the ocean teaches us that this is an illusion. The truth is that abundance is all around us. We may not always see it, but it is there, just as the deep currents of the ocean move beneath the surface, unseen yet powerful. The more we tune into this truth, the more we can let go of fear and trust in the natural abundance that surrounds us.

As you continue to meditate on this idea of limitlessness, reflect on the ways in which abundance shows up in your life. It may not always appear in material forms. Sometimes abundance is the love of family, the beauty of nature, or the peace that comes from within. Just as the ocean's abundance takes many forms, so too does the abundance in your life. It is always there, waiting to be recognized and appreciated.

In the end, the ocean reminds us that abundance is not about having more, but about recognizing the endless flow of life, of which we are already a part. There is no need to grasp or hold on tightly to what we have; instead, we should let it go. Like the ocean, we can trust that life will continue to provide, that we will always be supported, even when the tides of life seem uncertain.

As you finish this meditation, take a moment to feel gratitude for the abundance in your life. You are connected to this vast, limitless energy, and it sustains you in ways you may never fully understand.

The ocean's abundance is your abundance, and as you move through life, you can trust in its endless flow, knowing that you are always supported, always nourished, always part of something greater than yourself.

Chapter Nine

Meditation on Infinite Potential

A s you stand at the edge of the ocean, gazing out at its vast horizon, you are reminded of its sheer immensity. No matter how far you travel, you will never reach its end. Even with all the tools and technology we possess, we have only scratched the surface of its depths. The ocean is a world unto itself, as vast and mysterious as the universe, constantly renewing, regenerating, and revealing new wonders. This endlessness, this infinite potential, mirrors the potential within each of us: the possibility for growth, renewal, and discovery that lies beyond what we can see or imagine.

In meditation, we are invited to connect with this sense of infinite potential. We can recognize that this same potential exists within us.

Just as the ocean cannot be fully explored or contained, neither can our capacity for growth, creativity, or transformation be fully understood or contained. We, too, are constantly evolving, capable of renewing ourselves, learning, and expanding beyond the limits we place on our own minds and hearts.

Begin by closing your eyes and envision yourself floating on the surface of the ocean. Beneath you lies an entire world, so deep, so vast, that it stretches beyond your understanding. You cannot see all that exists below, but you know it is there. The ocean holds within it an infinite number of possibilities, from the smallest creatures to the largest currents, from the known to the unknown. The ocean is a reminder that potential is not something fixed or finite; it is endless, waiting to be discovered and explored.

As you breathe in, feel the expansive nature of the ocean filling your lungs. With each breath, you are tapping into this infinite potential, connecting to the energy of renewal and possibility. Just as the ocean regenerates itself, you, too, have the ability to renew and regenerate. Every breath, every moment, is an opportunity to tap into your own infinite potential, to explore the vastness within yourself that remains unexplored.

The ocean's potential is so great that even the most advanced technology cannot fully access it. We have sent submarines to its depths, mapped its surface, and explored its currents, but the majority of the ocean remains a mystery, untouched by human beings. This reflects the truth about ourselves: no matter how much we know or how far we go, there is always more to discover, more to learn. Our potential, like the ocean, is infinite, extending far beyond the boundaries we imagine for ourselves.

In life, we often place limits on ourselves, believing that we have reached the end of what we can do, learn, or feel. But the ocean teaches us that these limits are illusions. We are never finished growing; there is always more to explore and uncover. In meditation, we can begin to dissolve these self-imposed boundaries, allowing ourselves to expand into the infinite possibilities that life has to offer.

As you finish this meditation, take a moment to feel gratitude for the ocean's reminder of infinite potential. Its vastness, its mystery, and its ability to regenerate and create reflect the limitless nature of life itself. You, too, are part of this great cycle of renewal and possibility. Just as the ocean never reaches its end, neither do you. You can trust in the endless flow of energy, creativity, and growth that is always available to you.

CONCLUSION

A S YOU REACH THE end of this journey through the wisdom
of the ocean, take a moment to reflect on the lessons it
has shared with you. From the constancy of the waves to the
infinite potential that lies within its depths, the ocean has offered
us insights that are both profound and simple. It has reminded
us of the interconnectedness of all life, the gentle adaptability
needed to face obstacles, and the abundance that flows through all
things. The ocean's wisdom is timeless, and through meditation,
we can continue to return to these teachings whenever we need
grounding, renewal, or peace.

Each meditation in this book is an invitation to explore a different
facet of the ocean's vastness, whether that be its ability to nourish,
respond, regenerate, or traverse life's challenges with grace. These reflections are not just about the ocean but about life itself. The ocean's
rhythms mirror our own inner cycles, reminding us that we, too, are
part of something much greater than ourselves. May you find peace,
clarity, and connection in its timeless rhythms, and may the ocean's

boundless wisdom continue to inspire and sustain you on your journey.

LET THE OCEAN'S WISDOM RIPPLE OUTWARD

W HEN WE GIVE SOMETHING from the heart, without expecting anything in return, it brings peace, joy, and connection. Just like the ocean gives and gives, always flowing, always offering, we too can give in simple, powerful ways.

Would you help someone who is feeling lost, stressed, or disconnected?

Please leave an honest review of this book wherever you purchased it, to help another reader, or give a copy as a gift.

Your words and actions might help...

...one more reader pause and breathe.

...one more heart soften with the tide.

...one more spirit remember its vastness.

...one more soul reconnect with nature.

Thank you for helping the ocean's message reach farther. May your own heart feel the same calm and care you give to others.

With gratitude,

Claudia E. Moore

ABOUT THE AUTHOR

CLAUDIA E. MOORE IS a lifelong lover of meditation and the ocean who believes that nature holds the wisdom we need to live more peacefully and presently. Blending mindfulness practices with poetic reflection, Claudia creates calming, accessible experiences for people who crave a deeper connection to themselves and the world around them. She is also an active memoirist whose captivating writing inspires readers to tap into their inner strength and embrace life with humor and resilience.

When not writing, reflecting, or crafting, Claudia can be found walking coastlines and forests, listening closely to the language of the natural world around us.

Ocean Reflections is her invitation for you to slow down, breathe deeply, and receive the quiet teachings of the sea.

You can follow her literary output at ClaudiaMooreScribe.com